MW01482766

Sold Out!

Top Event Marketing Strategies
to Create Social Media Buzz
for Your Next Event

Susan Ordona

loss or damage that may be incurred, or alleged to have been incurred, directly or indirectly, arising out of the information provided in this book.

The information herein is offered for informational purposes solely, and is universal as so. The presentation of the information is without contract or any type of guarantee assurance.

This publication is designed to provide general information regarding the subject matter covered. However, laws and practices often vary from state to state and country to country, and are subject to change. Because each factual situation is different, specific advice should be tailored to the particular circumstances. For this reason, the reader is advised to consult with his or her own advisor regarding that individual's specific situation.

The author has taken reasonable precautions in the preparations of this book and believes the facts presented in the book are accurate as of the date it was written. However, neither the author nor the publisher assumes any responsibility for any errors or omissions. The author and publisher specifically disclaim any liability resulting from the use or application of the information contained in this book, and the information is not intended to serve as legal, financial, medical, personal or other financial advice related to individual situations.

The trademarks that are used are without any consent, and the publication of the trademark is without permission or backing by the trademark owner. All trademarks and brands within this book are for clarifying purposes only and are owned by the owners themselves, they are not affiliated with this document.

Dedication

To my loving husband, Roger, and my dearest son, Andrew

To many of you who have touched my life
in so many different ways
and to those that I hope
will be inspired by this.

Table of Contents

Forward
By Emma Tiebens

Four years ago, on a beautiful San Diego afternoon, I sat on a picnic bench at a 5-star resort's grounds to enjoy my lunch. I was attending a conference where hundreds of marketing experts converged to learn and leverage video marketing. As I savored the serenity of the moment, I saw a lady walking towards me with a big smile on her face. My first thoughts were, "Oh my gosh, do I know her? I can't remember where I met her." We started talking and realized that we were both from the Philippines. Within minutes, we were sharing food and wonderful stories, took our selfies – way before people even knew what a selfie was- and we made a conscious decision to stay in touch.

I had barely gotten back to my seat at the event and I was getting notifications from all of my social media platform that I had been "tagged" and people were commenting on my photos. What photos? The photos Susan Ordona took of us went up and generated online engagement within minutes!

That's just how Susan is. Creating a big buzz for people, places, and philanthropy is her passion. When I had my very first live event in 2013, I needed someone to help me fill the seats and Susan immediately stepped-up, and within days, my event had sold-out!

I got to know Susan through the years and I watched her generate big buzz for many events through her masterful knowledge of the cutting edge technologies, leveraging them and integrating them in social media as well as traditional media.

She is what I would call a "Buzz Builder" because she truly is great at what she does!

Susan was born to write this book. She has the ability to connect with everyone she meets at a different level. She absolutely cares and wants her client's events to become successful – she absolutely delivers results!

While you may not be able to take Susan everywhere with you, she has written this highly detailed and simplified blueprint on how you too can create a big social media buzz for your events!

Susan has helped hundreds of icons, business mentors, speakers, authors, event producers, and coaches, and she can do the same for you! If you have read it this far, buckle your seat belts up because your life is about to change.

- Emma Tiebens,

Speaker, Media Host, and Bestselling Author of *Magnetic Memorable and TRUSTED*. www.EmmaTiebens.com

Forward
By Larry Loik

Susan (Suzie) Ordona—what a lady!

I met Susan and her husband, Roger, in 2006 in Orlando, Florida at one of our Real Estate Tours. The moment I met her, she offered to take me to the airport, which was out of their way. I was a total stranger to her, yet she asked for zero in return. That's Susan! I call her "Mother Theresa" because she always puts others first before herself.

I am honored that she asked me to write a foreword to this book. I could go on for many pages, but will save that for another time.

The thing about Susan is that she knows everyone and supports everyone. Because of her kindness, she has spent a lot of her time promoting others without concentrating on sharing her own gifts and talents with the world. I have been "pushing" her to create a product or book for years, and I'm proud that she has finally gotten her word out.

"Ms. Susan," as the Filipinos call her, has been promoting our online and offline events for years, helping us fill them via social media and her vast networking at live events.

Susan has grown to be a family friend over the last few years. She has been there for me during my most down times, despite her having down times of her own.

She is a self-proclaimed "Social Media-Holic" and knows social media inside and out. In addition, she has attended so many live events that she is definitely a "Seminar Junkie."

Times have changed: with the Internet, live-streaming webinars, traffic, people's time, and the economy, live events worldwide typically have seen lower attendance compared to a few years ago. Having been involved as an attendee, marketer, and speaker at live events, "Ms. Susan" knows every angle and strategy to create the social buzz and to fill seats.

I highly recommend that you read this book cover to cover and take lots of notes to act on. It will help you not only fill your event but also put on a memorable event that your attendees will talk about for years (and refer more people to future ones).

Next time you see her at a live event, thank her and give her a hug. You'll be glad you did.

Larry Loik

Complete Marketing Systems Inc Las Vegas NV USA
www.dropshipquick.com

Introduction

Congratulations for taking action by reading my book on how you can have a "sold out" event!

Among the many reasons why you purchased my book is most likely that you're a speaker, author, consultant, expert, event producer, or an event organizer. Maybe you have held events before and want more ways to promote your next events. You could be someone who is thinking of holding your own event in the future but is uncertain about where to start! Maybe you are someone who would like to help people create their own events, but you are not sure what to do!

As you see on the title of my book, at the end it says, "For Your Next Event" because whether you have had an actual live event or not, you certainly have "that" event in your mind that is waiting to materialize. Well, the time is now.

This book was designed to help anyone wanting to produce events, large or small. I have included insights and information that you can use whether you are self-producing and have a low-budget for marketing or if you have a full team of people supporting you.

Whatever reasons you have for why you picked up this book, event marketing by social media buzz cannot be ignored anymore. Online and offline marketing strategies are integrated to get the maximum results and that is the beauty of social media!

As you read my book, you'll be led to a roadmap by your guide, me!

My name is Susan Ordona, and I'm here to take you on a tour navigating the landscape of creating the social media buzz for your event marketing so you can fill those seats, get your events to sell out, spread your reach with your event's messages to the world, and who knows, you might just change someone's life - all because of your event!

Nine years ago, if you would have asked me about marketing, I probably would have had a strange look on my face. You see, my career was in the health-care as a Clinical Laboratory Scientist. My line of work was behind the scenes - nothing about being in a social work environment. I didn't know anything about business or entrepreneurship, and social media was not even a common term! However, one thing I have always known is that I am a very social, outgoing person who loves to go to parties, be with people, meet new friends, and have good clean fun.

Nine years ago, I had a self-discovery and reinvented myself following my passion in business and being an entrepreneur. In addition to my desire and eagerness to learn something new mostly in self development and find some answers to some of my life's questions, I expanded my learning from reading and watching motivational videos to attending live events...until I got hooked. My quest for learning expanded to more and more event topics that included not only motivation and personal development but also real estate, internet marketing, speaking, outsourcing, book writing, social media and many more. These are in addition to my continuing education in Laboratory Medicine through live and virtual events.

I became a "seminar junkie" (in a good way), attending seminars, conferences, workshops, bootcamps, retreats, webinars; thus meeting, learning and being inspired by thought leaders, visionaries, innovators, and speakers that if I named them all here, their names will fill my whole book.

The more I went to live events, I more I noticed how each event was being promoted. How did I get there? What motivated me to attend the event? What interested me about the event? Why did I choose a particular event to attend? Should I attend another event by the same organizer or should I skip next time? Why would I do that? Was it worth my time? These are the questions I had as an attendee.

I started to observe and take notes on what I liked and what didn't work about the events I attended. I studied their marketing strategies, especially as social media was getting more and more popular. And with that also comes the investment of time, money, and effort in learning about the constantly changing field of social media.

I was able to apply everything I learned:

- How to plan an event

- How to set up an event

- How to promote and market an event

- How to man the registration table

- How to be a greeter

- How to be the hospitality person

- How to act as customer service

- How to sometimes just be a friend to an attendee

- How to being a photographer and a videographer

- How to be a social media marketing strategist, a social media manager, and a social media correspondent

- How to just be there to listen, learn, and make friends!

Social media is so natural for me because I have been studying, learning, and researching this field ever since it became known as social media. Quickly, people started asking me questions and sought my advice.

Eventually, I became the "best-kept secret" as a Social Media Event Marketing Strategist and as a Social Media Correspondent at live events to some of the world's high profile Speakers, Experts, Authors, Consultants, Event Producers and Organizers in helping them create the Social Media Buzz for their live and virtual events.

I have learned so much over the years from the people I've met along the way. These are people that I have been blessed to have crossed paths with; they have inspired and enriched my life.

Now I would like to share with you the lessons I've learned. I love to learn the easy way, so I laid out the entire event marketing strategies as simply as can be so that it is easy to follow.

You might find that there are many tools, tips, and strategies in both offline, online, and integrated marketing processes here. Don't be overwhelmed. Just use the ones you need that align with your goal of having your event in the first place. It will also depend on some factors like the size of your event, your target audience, the time you have to promote your event, your budget, your manpower...among others.

It is my hope that you'll have the confidence to promote your events like the pros do by using the strategies in this book in such a way that, whether you have a big team or just a handful, you'll find them doable and easy to implement.

So let's get started!

Chapter One:

Live Events -
The Basics

Why Do People Hold Events?

It's human nature to be social. We love to be with people who share our common interests, and events have always been a big part of our everyday lives. So whether it's a birthday party, a wedding, graduation party, anniversary party, a milestone for an entrepreneur, a seminar, conference, workshop, educational lecture, continuing education, symposium, a fundraiser, or a networking event, we love to hang out with people—something we do at all kinds of different events!

There are so many reasons why people love to hold and attend events. Not only are they for fun, satisfying our social cravings to be with people with whom we have common interests, but they are also one of the best tools available for growing your business; events can enhance marketing, build deeper relationships with your existing communities, and help you network with people who might become friends, clients, or customers.

There is no better time in our social world than now! Now more than ever, we are bombarded with invitations to different kinds of events. I used to receive invitations and find out about events by mail, phone, email, word of mouth, flyers, magazines, TV and radio. Nowadays, in addition to those forms of communication, we have the power of online reach.

I don't have to look any farther than my Facebook page to see evidence of this. Every day, I get a Facebook invite for an event, in addition to all the other ways I mentioned above. Event invites also happen every day on other social media networks.

In this book, I'll focus on live business events: seminars, conferences, workshops, bootcamps, summits, trade shows, classes, lectures, retreats, fundraising, trade shows, and trainings—in other words, any event where there is in-person physical interaction.

Why Live Events?

Live events have always been popular. They are the favorite choice of event planners, event organizers, and event promoters who seek to get that competitive advantage in business. They can take your business relationships to the next level with your existing clients and introduce you to new or potential customers. The main purpose of having event marketing is getting qualified attendees to your events.

Live events also help to introduce your brand if you are just starting. If you already have a brand, live events can strengthen your brand awareness. Most of all, your attendees get to see you as a live, real person and get to experience you as a leader and a person of influence!

What people learn from attending these events can be priceless, from affecting their mindsets to improving and changing their lives—it's all there in the key messages at these events!

What Do We Experience at Live Events?

It's a great feeling when we go to live events because we have the opportunity to interact with people in real life, not just online. We get to know our attendees better by gathering everyone together, connecting and reconnecting with friends and business contacts. Attending live events also gives us that extra jolt of energy—when I go to an event, as I listen to the speakers and their topics, I'm thinking, "Wow! These are messages with information that could change people's lives!"

If you have been interacting with people on Facebook, Twitter, or Instagram, live events should definitely be in your business plan; they'll provide you with a means of deepening those online relationships even further. It always amazes me when I go to live events and recognize my online friends in person! This gives me the opportunity to see my virtual friends, followers, circles, and connections and meet the real people behind the computer screens.

Most of all, live events are platforms to create that unique experience for your clients, your future clients, and your staff. It's the experience—particularly the feeling of how our senses react to the experience—that will determine whether your attendees will come to your next event, whether they will tell their friends, and even if they'll do business with you.

Why Do Events Play an Important Role in Your Marketing?

What's the percentage of business people who use live events as an important part of their businesses? It's 79%, according to findings on Constant Contact, so event marketing has to be in place. You've probably seen small or big live events and how they were sold out (or not) depending on the kind of event. Nevertheless, small or big, an amount of event marketing was done to attract the target audience.

Of course, we like to aim for sold-out live events. These could include everything from a very small, intimate gathering, to a medium-sized class, to a big conference with a few hundred people.

Imagine if you had an event, planned really well, and everything was perfect—but no one knew or heard about it. Successful live events don't just happen—they take a lot of work, effort, time, and money. It's a tough market out there! Live events are popping up every day, and people are bombarded with more choices than ever before. Event organizers, including speakers, authors, experts, consultants, and coaches, are faced with a lot of challenges. Even if they have a system in place for attracting people to their events, they still struggle to compete and get people to their events.

It's very clear why live events have to be included in your marketing strategic plan. Live events give you the opportunity to market to many people at once, instead of marketing to one person at a time, depending on how specific you want your event to be.

Events: How Showing Up Will Impact Your Business

> "80% of success is showing up."
> — Woody Allen

He must have read my mind when he said this! I am one of those that show up at events most of the time. I call myself an event junkie in a good way. It must be the social side of me, my love of people, the excitement, the noise, music, bustle, chatter, loudspeakers, that makes me want to be there and have that experience. Most of all, it is about all kinds of interactions that we have when we participate in these events.

Events are usually thought of as live events, but from a business point of view, events are not only face-to-face events as expos, trade shows, workshops, conferences, and seminars, but also online events as well like webinars and teleseminars.

Why do we even bother to attend these gatherings? It doesn't matter if there are two people or 1,000 present. Either way, you get to engage, connect, communicate, and deepen your relationships with people, whether you are in educational lectures, promotional product demonstrations, open houses, fundraisers, board meetings, or on webinars.

Over the few years that I have been going to events, offline and online, I have met, listened to, and shared ideas with wonderful people that I have developed friendships as well as business connections. The learning experience, the education, knowledge, and the take-aways are just so priceless. There is always something, no matter how small, that you learn every time.

One of the challenges though is answering these questions: What event should I go to? Where do I find an event that I will like? What about one that will help me meet my goals, especially in business?

Keep in mind that events could help you with new perspectives in your businesses with the new ideas, technology, joint venture possibilities, tons of clients and customers, and a lot of other benefits as well.

Chapter Two:

Live Event Marketing - First Things First

What Are The Challenges of Event Marketing?

Attention to detail is crucial when planning events. Start with a very basic plan: list your event's What, Why, Where, When and How. These are important to you as you plan, but how you execute the plan is even more important to your attendees.

Never lose sight of attending to details throughout the event process. From the time your event was just a thought until after it's over, there will be a lot of moving parts, and you'll have a lot on your plate. By attending to details, you'll be better able to work your way through the challenges of planning your event, marketing your event, and the after-event process.

Budget - How to Be Cost Effective

As an event planner or organizer, you must know your overall budget for the event. As an event marketer, you should plan for at least 20% of your event funds to go to marketing. Determining that will help you a lot in moving forward with your event. Marketing is just one big part of your event process; in addition to that, you still have to tend to the venue rent, food, and other expenses.

Make sure you have a good picture of your budget from the very start. You definitely don't want to be at the end stages before the event and find out that you don't have enough funds to pay the photographer, the DJ, the videographer, or your social media manager.

Time

Time management and awareness is essential to planning a successful event. Make sure you know the answers to the following questions as you begin planning.

- How much time do you have to plan the event? How much time do you have for marketing the event?

- Do you have enough time to get your event's word out to the world?

- Have you set up a detailed timeline for the different aspects of your event?

- What would be an ideal timeline for planning and marketing your event to existing and new attendees?

- What would be an ideal timeline for planning and marketing your event to your existing communities and social media networks?

Logistics

Although this book is not about event planning itself, it is a very important part of the whole process. It's funny; when I tell people that I create the social media buzz for event marketing, they usually assume I am an event planner.

This is where we attend to the what, where and when. What needs to be addressed? Where is the venue? When is the event? These are all questions that you have to answer. Think about the event location, date, food, networking party, etc.

Crowdsourcing plays a role here because you could be asking friends, family, neighbors, people you know, co-workers, and business partners for recommendations for event locations, hotels, entertainments, restaurants, points of interest, health facilities, hospitals, etc.

Set a deadline for every step of your planning and marketing, that way you'll have a clear picture of where you are in the process.

Event Planning and Marketing Team

The size of your event team will depend on the size of your event, the type of your target audience, and the topics of your event. Who will be doing what? Will you be doing most of the tasks, or do you have a team?

This is a team of people that every event organizer should have if at all possible. Roles may overlap. Depending on the size of your event and the time involved, you may be able to combine some of these tasks with each other.

1. Overall event organizer/ admin/go-to-person—will be overseeing the whole operation. 2) Event planner—will be in charge of all logistical needs such as the venue, catering, entertainment, and parties.

2. Copywriter—will help to write blog posts, articles, website sales copy and marketing language for print materials.

3. Web designer or a website builder

4. Graphic designer

5. Content curator

6. Researcher

7. Photographer

8. Videographer

9. Social media marketing strategist/social media manager/social media correspondent/social media command center

10. Blogger

11. Volunteers

Example of young entrepreneurs volunteering like this at Emma Tieben's HardSell2HeartSell live event. Charley Mae Nocete, my niece and Garrett Tiebens, Emma's son, were helping out at the registration table and acted as greeters.

Competition

We are seeing that events are increasingly becoming a big part of strategies for all kinds of businesses. You should make sure to incorporate them into your business as well, no matter how large or small.

As I mentioned in the beginning, I get a lot of invites on Facebook (along with Google+ and LinkedIn), and I'm sure you do too. It's undeniable that there is a lot of competition for our attention, along with every one of the 1.35 *billion* Facebook monthly users! It's a tough market out there, with live events popping up every day, so as marketers and event producers, we're up against all kinds of challenges in our events. Keep focused on your tasks and you'll lay the foundation for a successful event.

Chapter Three:

Finding Your Audience

Who is Your Target Audience?

What are some of the challenges you might face when you think about your target audience? Here are a few:

- That first attempt to make them notice your invitation, as you're competing with a number of event invitations that people are faced with every day. On Facebook alone, I get a minimum of two invites a day. There's quite a lot of noise out there. How do you stand out? By creating something of value that's relevant and will get the attention of your ideal target audience. Use keywords in your marketing pieces that are specific for the industry or your niche topics.

- Attracting people to your invitations.

- Getting them to respond to your invites.

- Making sure that they hit the "register" button once they respond.

- Avoiding "no-shows"—sometimes even when people register for the event, they still won't show up. This is what some organizers do, especially when it's a free event: charge a refundable fee upon registration. When attendees show up at the event, they get refunds back to their accounts; otherwise they get charged.

- Determining exactly how many people are coming—send consistent reminders! A day before and/or the day of the event, call or designate someone to call the registrants by phone to remind them about your event.

- Don't leave non-responders out of your marketing process. They may not be ready now, but maybe they will be for your next event.

I used to attend every event I liked, whenever I could, about topics including personal development, internet marketing, real estate, speaking, book writing, book self-publishing, networking events, drop shipping, eBay, social media, network marketing, and continuing education. I'm quite experienced at being a target audience member!

Step Into Your Audience Shoes

To understand more about what goes on the minds of your prospects, ask some questions and put yourself in the shoes of your clients or potential attendees. These are the questions that I ask myself, ones that you should ask yourself too:

- What's the event about?
- What are the topics?
- Is it relevant to what I'm doing at this moment?
- Who are the speakers?
- Who is sponsoring this event?
- Who is attending?
- Which of my friends or network are going?
- Will there be exhibitors?
- Do I like and trust the organizers?
- Is it a free or paid event?
- Is it a local event, or will I have to travel?
- If I have to stay in a hotel, do they have discounts?
- Where is the event going to be?
- What's the expense involved?
- How many days is the event going to be?
- Will there be networking?
- Have I attended this event before, or is this the first time?
- Do I have the time to attend?

If the answers are a good fit, depending on their needs, then they would more than likely attend your event.

As I've said, I've been to many events in the last few years, learning a great deal, meeting many wonderful people who have become my friends, and applying those lessons to my life and business. I am an ideal client or event attendee, just like those of you who have been to live events. I am the event organizer's target audience! Who's your target audience?

Your Audience Finding YOU

How Will They Find Me?

There are a myriad of ways for your audience to find you. What has worked for me are the following:

- I'm on their email lists
- I liked their Facebook Business fan page
- I'm connected with them via LinkedIn
- I follow them on Twitter
- I'm in their Google+ circles
- I'm their Instagram friend
- I'm their Pinterest follower
- I'm their Youtube subscriber
- They called me on the phone
- Sent me direct mail or postcard
- I might have seen them on TV
- Heard of them on the radio

- Met them at an event

- Saw them on an event flyer

- Heard about them from a friend

I love attending events for different reasons and that has also helped me become more visible, not only to my target audience but for qualified collaborators who are global thinkers and movers and shakers in their own right.

As I expand my success network, guess what? I am also becoming visible to my ideal audience! This is one of the secrets to honing in to your ideal audience. By having a powerful presence online and offline, I am creating instant rapport and almost immediately they get to know me, like me and more importantly, trust me.

Now let's reverse the roles. Think about events you've attended. What are the common desires by the attendees? What did they want to achieve by attending these events? This is your "least common denominator" – these are the things that are important to all of you. These are going to attract your ideal audience to resonate with you.

Now let's imagine this for a moment. You are the event organizer and you want to reach your target audience. Where and how do you find your target audience?

First, you have to decide who your target audience is for your live event. When you know who you're marketing to, it will be easier to tailor your event's details, including topics, format, and duration.

Ask Your Audience

Ask those same questions you asked yourself earlier, from the perspective of your potential attendees. Then, look at the existing communities you already participate in. These are the networks that you already have relationships with and have continuing engagement. Start with your existing Fan Base, your Email database or list, your friends, followers, connections, circles, and subscribers in those social media networks because they already know you, like you and trust you. Listen to the conversations going on. Listen to what their interests are. You might even do a survey using a survey tool such as http://SurveyMonkey.com.

It is crucial to know what your target audience is interested in and what they want. Pattern your messages to offer something that they can identify with. If you do, you should end up with qualified attendees that are targeted specifically to what your event is all about.

Chapter Four

Event Planning 101

Imagine you are the organizer of an event. You have the perfect setting, the location is a very nice hotel, you have planned every little detail of the logistics of the event perfectly. The food, entertainment, environment, everything is in place, perfect beyond your wildest dreams. The event team or staff is there: your photographer, videographer, audio person, speakers, and volunteers. But sometimes things happen, and the worst is that only a few people have shown up. You have empty seats all over—not impressive on your event photos and videos. You've spent a lot of money on this.

What happened? Not many people knew about your event, or, if they did, they weren't motivated enough to click that "register" button. Your event was invisible to much of your target audience. What could you have done to gain more exposure for your event?

Here are some common reasons why you might have empty seats at your event:

- Invisibility

- Lack of exposure

- Lack of attendance

- Lack of marketing - Nobody knows about your event!

Results or consequences of a poorly attended event:

- Loss of revenue

- Loss of credibility and reputation

- Loss of time

- Loss of staff

So marketing your event is crucial!

Here is where we start our marketing efforts:

1. Save The Date

Save The Date: Three very important words in event marketing! This phrase is the very first one you send to all your contacts and connections. Once you have a date, tell the world about it so people can put in their calendars, arrange work and family schedules, and have it in their minds. If there are any changes, be sure to let the world know about it in a timely manner so they can adjust schedules accordingly. The earlier you get this message to all the people you want to be at your event, the better chances you have of having them there. People are so bombarded with so much information that your being on top of their minds is a good thing.

To do:

- Create an image of the Save The Date using a free tool like www.shareasimage.com (there are others out there, but this is my favorite). With this you can also put a text of your own website on the image.

- I always want everything to come from the main business website, so writing a blog about your Save The Date would be the most logical thing to do. Since you want to tell the world about it anyway, why not post a blog or an article about it? Be sure to embed the image in your blog post. You can also send this blog post in your emails and your email newsletter.

- From your website, you can post the link to your Facebook, Twitter, LinkedIn, pin it to Pinterest, Google +.

- Create a very short video using www.animoto.com. Post on Youtube and share to social media networks.

2. Clarify Event Mission and Message

Clarity is a very important first part of your event planning and marketing. Without that, your roadmap is going to be blurry and you won't be able to see clearly where you're going with your event. Ask yourself why you're doing what you're doing.

- How much of your time do you want to take out of your personal life to take on a project like this?

- What do you want to get out of this?

- Do you have a buffer if you need one?

- Do you have an exit strategy just in case?

- How clear are you with the topics you want to share at your events?

- How about the speakers?

- Do you have their contact information background?

- How well do they fit your criteria to deliver the message?

Those are some questions that you have to ask yourself to get clarity.

3. Find the Venue

Finding the venue or location of your event is challenging as there are many pieces of information needed to find the "perfect" location. Some events have event planners that will

SOLD-OUT!

take care of this part. They are part of your event planning team. There are cases where the event planner will be you!

So, what are the things to consider when looking for a venue?

To determine the size of the venue, know how many attendees you'll have.

- Are those attendees from the area or not? If they are local, most likely they won't need rooms to stay overnight. If they are from out of town, then they need hotel rooms. Be ready to refer nearby hotels if needed.

- How many people are in your staff? Depending on the number, the venue matters. You need more room to move around if there's a number of you plus the speakers, of course. Will there be a place for your registration table inside the venue or outside the door?

- How about you, as the event organizer, do you live in the area of your event or do you have a long way to travel? If the venue is closer to your home, it will be very convenient for you.

- Will there be Wi-Fi connection? On the section of "During Event" on Chapter Seven, I stress the importance of Wi-Fi connection during the event. You'll have people that will want to use the internet to do social media sharing for your event.

- Does the venue provide a stage for the speakers? Is there enough space? Do you need to rent a stage or not?

- Is there an adjacent room especially for speakers and staff? That's a sort of a break room for your staff and also for the speakers.

- Is the venue in a hotel? If so, it will be very convenient for out of town attendees.

- Your seminar attendees will most likely be hungry. Is there a restaurant at the venue? Do attendees have to travel?

- Is there a bar or a small lounge that attendees can hang out after the seminar?

- How far are the airport, the train station, and the bus stops from the venue?

- Is there any shuttle to the nearest airport?

- Are there enough electric outlets for audio/visual equipment?

- Is the venue going to offer breakfast or do attendees have to go outside to get something to eat?

- Does the venue offer water, coffee, tea or some snack bars?

- How about for lunch? Does venue offer quick lunches like brown bag light lunches?

- Will attendees have access to a business office with computers, printers and fax machines?

- Is there some kind of entertainment facility where attendees can go to unwind after a long day at the seminar?

- For the sports minded people, is there a gym or a swimming pool available to attendees?

- Will there be a front desk that will provide information on the nearby facilities for dining, entertainment, and attractions?

- Is the venue easy to find? I've been to events where there are no signs, and with too many corridors and corners, it's confusing. If it's hard for you to find the room, it will be harder for your attendees to find your venue.

- How about parking? Is there ample parking? Is it free, discounted or full price? Sometimes lack of parking will turn people away. If they have to park on the street and walk one to two blocks to get to your event, they will just leave.

- Have you inquired if there are any events happening at the same time as yours? Many times I have gone to events, and we couldn't hear the speaker talking since there was a wedding with loud music next door!

4. Plan Your Event Format

This is going to be layout or mind-map of your event. This would include your event timeline, your deadlines for different tasks, assignments of tasks, event goals, marketing materials needed, and resources to get those materials from, catering, and even the layout of the event room itself.

Have a clear picture of this before you begin marketing.

5. Who Do I Need to Reach Out to for My Events?

1. Co-event producers - Instead of tackling all the responsibilities of holding an event by yourself, why not get a co-producer?

2. Speakers - You need to send invitations to them as early as possible. They have a very busy schedule, so it's better to communicate with them early on.

   I have done research on different speakers before for an event producer. First thing you have to find out is what the main topic of the event will be. Then find out who the speaker experts are on the topics. Are they local or not? It's easier to get a local speaker.

   You can delegate this research part to someone in your team.

3. Expert Panelists - These are speakers themselves that will be involved in panel discussion about your topics. You can have a few panels of speakers in different topics.

   A panel of 4-5 speakers is very common.

4. Sponsors and exhibitors - they are very important part of the event. The relationship between them and the event organizers is that of a win-win for both sides.

#1 REASON WHY BE A SPONSOR/EXHIBITOR AT A BIG EVENT: Large Exposure and Visibility to YOUR Company/Business to a highly-targeted audience..........Susan(Ask me "HOW"?)

susanordona.com

#2 Benefit: Sponsorships add instant credibility to your Company/Business being a leader and expert in the industry.

#3 Benefit: Sponsorships provide your Company/Business with a phenomenal opportunity to meet and interact with attendees who want to learn about your products and services.

susanordona.com

#4 Benefit: Sponsorships provide the platform for your Company/Business to be branded with the recognized names on the Speakers list.

susanordona.com

5. Exhibitors- similar to sponsors.

6. Circle of Influence/ Affiliates - Your circle of influence can really help share your event to their communities. Affiliates are also a big help. You can incentivize them by offering a percentage of commission for every event ticket they sell.

7. Volunteers - These are usually people who like to help out, or want to experience the event. They become part of the staff and are big assets to the organization. Just make sure to give them proper orientation.

8. Attendees - Since they are excited to be attending the event, they want to share it to their friends. Sometimes attendees could also be affiliates.

The Perks of Volunteering at Events

This was during the event "OUTSOURCE LIVE" by Global Lifestyle Entrepreneur and New York Times Best Selling Author, Daven Michaels at the LAX Westin Hotel Los Angeles, CA. (www.123Employee.com)

1. Attend the event for FREE ($1997 value)

2. 1-2 private group strategy sessions with Daven and his partner.

3. Paid parking for Fri. Sat. Sun.

4. 1 paid meal a day for Fri. Sat. Sun.

5. "Outsource Live" T-shirt

6. 1-2 books from the event

7. Attend a live performance

8. A promo video for your business (then learn how to monetize that from one of the speakers)

9. Daven Michaels – virtual business development specialist

10. Speaker 2 – Virtual business development specialist

11. Speaker 3 – Will show you how to monetize your video content

12. Speaker 4 – The fastest reader in the world will show you how to shortcut your learning and speed up your success

13. Speaker 5 – Will show you how to network and extract profits out of networking "groups"

14. Speaker 6 – Will share cutting edge technology to make webinars as tools to build your business

15. Meet all the fun-loving people who love to learn and experience an information packed weekend

16. NETWORKING to grow your business

What do I need to do?

- You promise to bring your smiles with you.

- You must be in a happy dancing mood.

SUSAN ORDONA

- You hi-five people as they come in.

- You help people in and out of the room.

- Be your happy, energetic self.

Chapter Five:

Assembling Your Social Media Marketing Team

Ideally, this would be as complete a marketing team as it could be. Then again, every event is different. Depending on several factors like budget, availability of people, skills, etc. this list could be short if one person can be performing one, two, or even three tasks sometimes.

1. **Photographer** - The photographer could be someone from your staff, a hired professional one, or you! He or she should take a lot of photos from the time of the event planning up to "after event." You, as the event organizer, should give clear, simple instructions to your photographer. Your expectations should be clearly defined.

If you have a professional photographer, make sure to be clear on who owns the rights to the photos.

Also, if you have a designated person doing the photography for your event, make sure that person knows what your expectations are. Provide this person with the camera to use. Maybe provide two just in case you need a backup.

2. **Videographer** - This is pretty much the same as above, except that this person takes videos. Again, if you have a professional videographer, be clear on who owns the rights to the videos.

3. **Graphic designer** - The graphic designer will combine art and different technologies or software to create your visual beautiful images you can use for your main website, event website, covers for your different social media networks, images for postings, and more.

4. **Web developer** - The web developer is the one who will create your websites. They will make sure that the design, graphics for your header, background, theme, features, functionalities, and that necessary plug-ins are installed. They also has to make sure that the ranking of your website in terms of SEO (search engine optimization) is taken care of. They will be responsible for maintaining the quality of your website.

5. **Copywriter** - The copywriter will be the one who will write all the written content like articles, blogs, press release, announcements, content for your website like "about" page, blurbs for social media postings, swipes for affiliates, tweets for Twitter, content for your event website, and more. Grammar, punctuations, and flow of the content are important.

6. **Social Media Event Marketing Strategist** - This is a social media professional who will lay out the social media marketing plan for your event. He/she will also ensure that everyone in the team is in the same page with regards to social media marketing. This person also has to communicate with the team on a consistent basis, and be alerted for any updates that he/she needs to know. For example: If there's a new speaker added to the speakers list, or a sponsor cancelled or an entertainment segment has been added to the event.

7. **Social Media Manager** - This person could be the same as the Social Media Strategist, depending on the size of the event. They could combine forces and help each other carry out the tasks. If there's more social media marketing to do, then it's better to have both. The social media manager will be doing a lot of implementation of the Social Media Marketing Strategy. This would include creating real time posts, deleting spam, be the customer service by answering questions, commenting, liking, monitoring and maintaining the social media networks that you're utilizing for the event, creating profiles, posting photos, videos, links to articles, and many more!

You, as the event organizer, have to provide this professionals all the materials they need for marketing your event, contents, timely information that relate to your event so they can publish accurate information.

8. **Social Media Correspondent** - What a Social media Correspondent (SMC) does is not so clear with a lot of people. An SMC does short, candid, on the spot, spontaneous video interviews of event participants during the event. He/she also does the social media (on site) live coverage of

your event mostly by video interviews, and with time permitting also taking photos, posting tidbits of your events online, and blog about your event.

Social media in action at a live event!

A social media manager should also be on hand to help upload that content to social media as soon as possible.

I know SMC is not a very popular job in events. I'll tell you why we should be seeing more and more of them at events.

Here are some reasons why Social Media Correspondents should be seen at events more:

1. People (attendees) always want to be part of an event. They want to get involved and what would be better than be on camera being interviewed about the event! SMCs make that happen!

2. You also make people feel special, more so if you have a "red carpet" setting. SMCs make it possible!

3. People want to be heard. SMCs listen!

4. Those candid, spontaneous, short videos are testimonials for you, the event organizer! SMCs are delivering those to you!

5. These short videos are done in real-time. You are creating excitement especially for those that are not at the event. When you're watching the Oscars, don't you feel excited when you see glimpses of the energy at the event? Those people (non-attendees) watching your real time videos could be your potential event attendees next time you have an event. People get excited about what's going on at the event when they see them live. SMCs make it happen!

6. Branding for your event! SMCs make it possible for you. When they interview someone in front of your event banner, what does that mean to you? More credibility for you and your event. There you go!

7. Come to think of it, your attendees are your celebrities! Your SMCs are celebrity creators as well.

8. There is a lot of overlap in all these roles of the social media teams, especially the three social media people. So, it's really up to you to define each person's role depending on the event's needs.

9. YOU - yes, you! You are the most important person in the Social Media Marketing Team. As the event producer or event organizer, you are the one conducting all the moving parts of the Social Media Marketing Team.

Chapter Six:

Ready...Set...Campaign

Here are the "foundation" steps that are very important to take as you set your event campaign stage, getting ready to start your full-blown event marketing campaign. These are key steps that you can use in any business, whether you have an event or not.

We will be talking about quite a few tools, strategies, tips, and techniques here. Don't be overwhelmed by possibilities: my purpose is just to lay them all out for you so you can pick and choose what you want to apply and implement in your event marketing campaign. On that note, let's focus on the most popular platforms and tools that are familiar to many.

1. Assess Your Online Inventory (Website, Blog, Email Marketing, Social Media, others) Make an inventory of your online and social media presence! Take note of what you have, what to focus on, and what you want to add to the mix. Do you have a website? An email marketing system? Are you active on social media? Decide what you want to keep, delete, and add.

Review your business's current online presence: your website, blog, branding, social media profiles, video marketing, and email marketing system, and determine what is working for you and what is not working. Evaluate how you can get the most out of your social media interactions, how you can consolidate your efforts and improve your online exposure.

2. Build or Refresh your Online Presence

Once you do your audit and know where you want to be online, set up your social media, your main business website, and your email marketing system. These are tools you want to explore and use for your marketing so your event online presence is established, so make sure the sites are designed properly and integrated with other networks. If you already have presence in some of them, refreshing the sites would be a good idea.

Main Business Website

You're probably wondering, "What does my website have to do with my event?" There are different ways that event organizers do this. One way is to incorporate your main business website with your event. Your event is going to be prominently displayed on your website. I'll show you where you can optimize your event on your main website.

While you're currently promoting your event, you have to make sure that your main business website is playing a role. This is especially beneficial when you can drive people to

your main website to find your event. It will be helpful even
when the event is over: people had a chance to visit your
website and you've hopefully won them over as subscribers.

Let's navigate the main website and how to optimize it to
showcase your event. Different places to find your event:

1. Website Header – This should have your event's logo or
banner. Make sure it's clickable, leads to your event's
page, and is prominent enough to be noticed when people
visit your main website.

   a. Banner/logo - with event name, location, date, and a
   call to action (CTA) like, "For more information,
   click here."

   b. Above the header, there's a plugin that you can install in
   your main website called "Hello Bar" plug-in. This
   should be strategically positioned so your website visitors
   can see your message right away. This plug-in allows you
   to create a call to action about your event.
   http://hellobar.com

   This is very helpful, especially when you have a webinar
   about your event—maybe an overview or a preview of a
   speaker's topic at your upcoming event. Here's an
   example of a call to action: "Register Here for the Event
   of the Year Preview Webinar." Once this is clicked, it
   will take the visitor to the webinar registration page,
   which would also lead to your event website.

   c. After the webinar, this Hello Bar plug-in can be
   modified to your main event. A call to action like

"Join 100+ Entrepreneurs at the Event of the Year" and will lead you the main event registration link.

2. Navigation Bar - You should have an "Event" page for people to check out what event you have coming up.

On your "Homepage" or your "Blog", social media sharing buttons should be put on each blog post so people can easily share your content.

3. Sidebar - Add social proof—feature on your main website some highlights from previous events (if you had any) on your main website so people will be able to see how those were conducted. That could be another clickable graphics/image for your event. It could also be your event video invitation or Social Media Sharing buttons.

Top Tip: Create a Blog post consistently, daily if possible!

Some Important Website Information

Recently, I was asked by a client what he could do to improve his online presence. So first thing I did was to ask him for his website URL. Even though I don't normally offer website building services, I usually look at client's website first before talking about social media services.

My client already has an existing website with the domain name and hosting.

I explained that a website is like his house, it is his. He owns his house. He bought his domain name and has it hosted by a hosting company.

Next, I asked if he liked his theme. Then plug-ins came into the picture after that.

What Is A Theme?

The simple answer I gave was this: A theme is like the design and layout of your house – including the colors, the fonts, the header, the background, and more.

What Are Plug-ins?

Plug-ins are like the furniture in a house, they add functionalities to the house.

The client's website definitely needed a makeover, so we started by changing the theme. Then we added more necessary plug-ins and deleted less needed ones.

There are so many themes out there. Which one do you pick? Well, it depends on the look that you want for your brand.

Event Website or Online Registration Sites

Your event website will be the main hub of all your event information in detail. It should have all the information a potential attendee will need.

Let's explore what you can do here. You don't need to have all of these features—it depends on what will work best for you. There are different ways to build your event website, from a very simple landing page to a robust, full website. You should be able to work something out with your web designer or web developer on your team.

Event name - at this time, you should have your event name selected, with a great keyword or keywords (for SEO [search engine optimization]) and a customized URL so your event can easily be found through a basic website search on the internet. You should have:

- Event theme
- Event Logo
- Event tagline
- Event site colors/fonts

1. Header

Just like at your main website, you should also have this plug-in installed on your event website, the "Hello Bar" plugin (http://hellobar.com) above the header. Include a call to action like "Click here to register for Event" or "2 more days before Event - Join now."

This plugin is also great if you have a webinar leading to the event itself. You can put a call to action here, like this example: "Register for the Event webinar." After the webinar, put back your main event's call to action.

You can have an event logo/banner with the event's name, date, location, and telephone number on your event's header graphic, or you can have the whole header display this information along with some social proof like "as seen on ABC, NBC, CBS, FOX, CNN, etc."

2. Navigation Bar — these are some of the pages on the navigation bar

    a. "About" page or "Homepage"—offers a full description of the event or a summary or overview of what the event is all about: who should attend, who it is not for, reasons why your event is different from others in similar niches, why people should attend, and your event's mission.

    b. Agenda or Schedule—this is a detailed schedule for the days of the event, including starting and ending times, room locations, who'll be speaking, topic descriptions, and break times.

    c. Speakers—this lists all the speakers' names, photos, bios, and topics.

    d. Sponsors—list all the event sponsors and their company descriptions.

    e. Exhibitors—list all the exhibitors and their company descriptions.

    f. Travel information—include a map of the city, a map to the venue, and directions from airports, train stations, or bus routes. Also, suggest transportation to other places like nearby restaurants, shopping malls, hospitals, car rentals, taxis, points of interests, limos, shuttles, public transportation, and internet connections.

    g. Hotel—address, telephone number, parking information, and recommendations for other hotels near the venue.

h. FAQs—frequently asked questions.

i. Networking Party—information about the networking party. This is a fun event that the event organizers plan for the attendees. Sometimes they are free, while at other times there is a charge.

j. Register button—very important. This is where the event fees are collected and the event attendee count is tracked. This should be prominently displayed on the website so it catches a viewer's attention easily.

k. Contact us—this is a sure way for people to contact the event team if they have questions. There will be questions no matter how complete you think your event web site might be.

3. Sidebar

a. Calendar widget—a visual reminder, a countdown to your event day or to a webinar, usually showing the days, hours, minutes, and seconds.

b. Testimonials—text, photo images, or videos from past attendees, speakers, sponsors, and exhibitors.

c. Highlights of past events—photos and videos.

d. Social media sharing buttons — very powerful, as these encourage connections, engagement and conversations.

Other ways include creating an event website or landing page by itself, or using an online event registration site like Eventbrite or Constant Contact's EventSpot.

Manage Your Online Presence

I recommend ongoing management and maintenance for a minimum of three months, regardless of the duration of your event campaign. Even after the event, you will need to continuously engage with your networks, including Facebook friends, Twitter followers, LinkedIn connections, subscribers, and other friends on other networks.

Chapter Seven:

Create The Buzz - Fill The Seats!

Why Social Media For Event Marketing?

According to research[1], 40% of businesses use social media for event marketing. That percentage could be even higher nowadays, since online marketing, especially with social media, is increasingly becoming heavily integrated with offline marketing. Social media has changed our way of communicating, our way of thinking, and our way of marketing our businesses, services, and products.

Social media is everywhere now, unlike a few years ago when it was just mainly for sharing personal photos with friends and family. Now, it's a whole different ballgame.

---

[1] "40% of Businesses Use Social Media for Event Marketing ..." 2014.
<http://blogs.constantcontact.com/40-of-businesses-use-social-media-for-event-marketing-ebook/>

Social media is a very inexpensive and cost-effective way to promote your events. Accounts on the various platforms are free to set up; you just have to know which ones you want to use.

As every target audience for every kind of event is different, your choice of social media platforms will also vary. So, choose the network that is relevant to your target audience. Meet them where they are!

Offline and Traditional Marketing Strategies - How Are They Social?

Have you ever received a flyer or a postcard in the mail about a seminar? Have you noticed that social media is in there too? Yes, it is, as you can see from the "Find us on Facebook" or "Follow us on Twitter" messages on the flyer or the postcard.

When you invite someone to your event via telephone, you probably say, "Please go to our Facebook Event page and register." You see all kinds of social media in almost all traditional marketing pieces now. The so-called traditional or offline marketing is intertwined now with social media, with a great deal of overlap in these marketing techniques. Some of the tactics here are still considered offline marketing, yet they contain an element of social media. For example, when you call a friend to invite to your event, it's offline, but then it becomes part of social media when you tell her that the event can also be found on Facebook.

What are the types of traditional of offline marketing?

- Email invitations and reminders Email newsletters
- Faxes
- In-person/Courier
- Bulletin boards Billboards Phone calls Flyers
- Word of mouth
- Direct mail
- TV
- Radio
- Newspaper
- Industry magazines or publications postcards

Social Media: It's All About The BUZZ!

Facebook

"Is Facebook still a great tool to promote my events?" That's a question that I get asked a lot, and my answer is always "Yes." Why not? According to statistics, in the US alone there are about 206.5 million unique monthly visitors to Facebook[2], and 1.35 billion people worldwide are active users[3].

With that many people, I am certain that most of the people I know are online and interacting on Facebook. Some even rely

[2] "comScore Ranks the Top 50 U.S. Digital Media Properties ..." 2015. <https://www.comscore.com/Insights/Market-Rankings/comScore-Ranks-the-Top-50-US-Digital-Media-Properties-for-February-2015>

[3] "Eight remarkable Facebook facts - CNBC.com." 2015. <http://www.cnbc.com/2014/04/24/seven-remarkable-social-media-facts.html>

on Facebook for private messaging instead of their emails. Facebook has become *the* most social of all social networks!

So, how do we get going on Facebook with our event marketing? The most popular way to do it is through an Events page. Here's a step-by- step guide on how to get there:

1. Go to your Facebook business Fan Page.

2. Add an "Events" app to your Fan Page.

3. Click on the "Events" tab. This takes you to a list of events you might have hosted in the past or are currently hosting.

4. Click on "Create Event"

5. You'll see a pop-up box which says, "Create New Event by Your Fan Page Name." Here you'll fill out the boxes with your event's information.

SOLD-OUT!

Facebook "Create Event"

- "Name": the name of your event - it should have keywords that are SEO- friendly so your event can be easily searched.

- "Details": this is the description of your event.

  o Since only the first 17 lines show up here by default when people come to your Event page, make sure your call to action like "REGISTER HERE" (in caps just because they attract attention) shows at least twice on that first fold.

  o Put the benefits of your event in bullet points for easier reading.

- o   At the bottom, put your call to action again.

- "Where": physical location or website (if it's a virtual event such as a webinar).

- "Tickets": this is a great feature: here you can put the direct link to your event's registration and allow attendees to get tickets for your event.

- "When": date of your event. You can just click on the calendar icon and choose the date.

  - o   Time: the time zone defaults to that of the location where this event page is originated, so it's important to stress this to your invitees. You can go the extra mile by determining the time zones of your target audience so there's no confusion.

- "Category": categorize your event by finding the closest one you see on the dropdown menu of the category. You'll notice that when you click and hover on those categories, sub categories appear. For example, when you click on "Interests," it gives you "conference" and "meet up" as sub-categories.

- Box: this says "only admin can post to the event wall." I leave that unchecked, as I want my attendees to be able to interact with me by being able to comment and post on the event page's wall. Otherwise, your attendees won't be able to engage with you regarding your event.

- "Select Targeting": this is a very narrowed target audience selection, which is very nice. When you click on the dropdown menu, it will show you target categories like Gender, Relationship Status, Educational Status, Interested in, Age, Location, and Language. You can narrow it down even further. For example, when you click on "Educational Status" it will segment it into "In High School," "In College," and "College Grad."

- "Create": then you can create (or cancel) your event.

- After you create your event, add an event photo.

  o The dimensions are the same as your Facebook cover photo (851 x 315 pixels). Select a nice cover photo that shows what your event is all about. This is prime marketing real estate here, so you want it to be visually appealing. Bear in mind that you should follow the 20% text rule, where text cannot exceed 20% of your cover photo size.

An Example of a Facebook Event page cover

For other ways to optimize your event page for marketing, let's take a look at the features on the event page. Here alone, there are a number of ways to promote your event.

1. "Public"—that's the default privacy setting for your event page, so it's visible to people on or off Facebook for much greater reach.

2. "Category"—it depends on what category you chose to narrow down the demographics of your target audience.

3. "Hosted by"—it will show that the event is hosted by your Facebook Fan Page (business), which is more exposure for your Fan Page.

4. "Join"—click that "join" button: you have to join your own event.

5. "Invite"—this is where you can invite your Facebook friends. If you've already created specific lists of friends (like personal or family friends), it's easy to just click once-- the invites go to all the people on the list. This saves you time instead of inviting people one by one, as long as all of those on the list are part of your target audience. –Otherwise, you can just select invitees one by one.

Facebook Event page "Invite" feature

6. "Invite"—some of the features you will see are the suggested invitees:

All Facebook friends - I'm sure you have many friends there who are also your business colleagues.

Selected Facebook friends

- Select Facebook lists - like family, close friends, co-workers, etc.

- In groups you belong to. Ask permission first.

- Your email contacts.

- Facebook friends who attended the same past Facebook event you've been to.

- Facebook friends who RSVP'd to the same Facebook event even though they did not attend.

- All invitees who RSVP'd to past Facebook events you hosted.

- You can also search for people on Facebook.

- You can also send private message invitations.

- On pages where you have an Admin role (if you're not the owner of the page, ask permission).

You can set your event either as public or a private event.

When you share a link, *always* say something about it, even if it's just one sentence. Encourage your friends to share the post to other people who would love to go to your event.

7. "Invite friends" - on the right hand side, Facebook gives you another avenue to invite your friends.

8. "Edit" - you can even edit your Event information. This is where you see the box at the bottom that says "Show guest list." I suggest that you check that box to show the guest list. Sometimes friends of friends go to your event if they see that *their* friends are going, and this could provide the opportunity to create a conversation on the event wall.

9. ... (those 3 dots mean "more") - when you click on this, it will take you to a dropdown menu:

Those three dots...

   A. Export event - where you can:

      a. Save to calendar

      b. Email it to yourself

B. Copy Event - you can create a copy of your event information. This is great if you have recurring events with the same themes and descriptions, only with different locations. This is a time saving tip.

C. Export the guest list - you can export the list to a file for easier access.

When you post your event on your Facebook Page, you can also "Boost Post"- this is a Facebook advertising tool, where you pay money for more targeted demographic marketing to extend your reach even more to your desired attendees.

Top Facebook Event Marketing Tips:

1. Remember that even if your invitees click on the "Join" button, it doesn't mean they're registered for your event. They have to go to the event details section to register on the registration link. You should post this registration link on the event wall every now and then, just to remind people about the link.

2. Don't forget the event hashtag!

3. Always welcome everyone who clicks the "join" button.

4. Create conversations.

5. "Like" each post, even if it's your own.

6. Comment on every attendee's post.

7. Designate someone (social media manager, if you have one) to monitor the conversations on your Event page, Your Fan Page, and on your personal profile.

8. Post consistently and often.

9. Don't forget to invite your speakers, sponsors, exhibitors, and panelists to your event page. Tag them. Encourage them to participate in the conversations so the attendees get to know them before the event.

10. Share your event on your personal Timeline for your family and personal friends. Remember 90/10 rule of thumb.

Engage, engage, engage!

Bonus Facebook Tip: How to edit a post after publishing it

For up-to-date information about features that you can use when sharing your event, visit my blog. Follow the link to learn more about editing your Facebook posts.

http://www.susanordona.com/new-facebook-feature-editing-your-post-after-publishing-it/

Linkedin

You probably won't think of LinkedIn as one of the top social media sites to promote events, but what if I tell you that with 414 million registered users worldwide, 92.7 Million of that are US based visitors that went to LinkedIn site[4].

---

[4] "• LinkedIn: numbers of members 2015 | Statistic - Statista." 2013. <http://www.statista.com/statistics/274050/quarterly-numbers-of-linkedin-members/>

LinkedIn is a social network for professionals and for people in business. You just have to know how to use the LinkedIn in a very effective way to be able to attract those businesses that are supporting your niche industries. These are your qualified attendees.

So, where do we start? How can we use LinkedIn for events?

1. Let's begin by looking at your LinkedIn profile. Your profile should position you as an expert in your industry. If you are an event host or organizer, say so on your profile as such without putting any links to your event.

   Make sure you have a profile photo. Don't just be a shadow. You've probably received an invite for LinkedIn connection only to be led to a faceless profile.

   If you have a photo, be sure it's professional looking.

   For your header (1400 x 425 pixel), use a high resolution image. Use your judgment in using your event images. With you on stage with your event logo in the background would be ok, as it's not the logo per se that you are showcasing, but it's yourself. You're positioning yourself as an expert, a person of influence especially in the events that you hold.

2. Join Linkedin Groups. Engage with your connections way ahead of time so you develop a relationship with the members for a while. With consistent group discussion participation, you'll have rapport with the members. Contact the group's manager and let him/her know about

your event, and go from there. Follow the group's rules and adhere to those. Remember always to be of value.

3. One powerful way to utilize LinkedIn is to create your own group specifically for your event. Reach out to all your speakers, panel experts, sponsors, exhibitors, circle of influence, staff, family and friends in business, attendees, your personal connections. Invite them to join the group. Create those business discussions. Promote your speakers. This could be a platform for them too to share their expertise relating to the topics that they will talk at your event.

4. You can also put your event on your postings by incorporating that in your regular updates. Be mindful when you're posting. It's always nice to write a sentence a two about your event and your event link, instead of just posting the link.

What you post on Facebook or Twitter may not be appropriate for a professional site like LinkedIn, so be careful with how you structure your posts.

5. You can send Invites to your LinkedIn connections. Just be mindful so you don't go beyond what is appropriate. I usually just send those invitations to the ones I know very well and ask them to share with their connections if they want to.

This is one strategy that I suggested to a very well LinkedIn connected speaker. The target audience was mostly on LinkedIn. So sending those connections a very

SOLD-OUT!

well thought of invitations to the event was the most strategic thing to do.

6. LinkedIn Pulse - another powerful way to let the world know about your event by publishing content about your event.

In order to get this, you have to install the InShare plug-in in your website, where your event site is integrated. Create a LinkedIn Company Page so you can associate your website to it.

7. Again engagement is the key. Create that connections and nurture them long before you have your event. It's better to be visible way ahead of time in a way that you have positioned yourself as a solution to what they're looking for and maybe lead them to follow you at your event.

8. LinkedIn Ads - you can always advertise your event through LinkedIn Ads. You can do this in addition to organic marketing strategies.

Twitter and Hashtag

When I think about Twitter, I think about sharing on social media in real time! I know, I know, here's another type of social media that we have to deal with in our event marketing process, but why not? With 320 million monthly active users[5], maybe there is something about Twitter that's worth looking at, especially when it comes to spreading news and information about your event.

[5] "Company | About - Twitter." 2013. <https://about.twitter.com/company>

71

Twitter is a very powerful platform for engaging, interacting, and connecting with your followers in real time. Thus, it's great for promoting your events at every stage, and most especially during the event. We'll talk about that later.

For now, let's dive into Twitter and look at our marketing real estate starting with our profiles.

Tips On Making the Most Out of Twitter for Event Marketing:

1. You can edit your profile by including your event website and event hashtag in the description box.

2. Your header image should measure 1500 x 500 pixels. Select an image that reflects your event, maybe a photo of you with your event banner in the background.

3. Grow your Twitter following. Follow your event participants and ask them to follow you back so you can engage in conversations. These could be those who are registered for your event, your speakers, sponsors, panelists, and your staff.

4. Twitter list - What groups are to LinkedIn, Twitter lists are to Twitter. It's a way to put all the people you're following on Twitter in one list. For example, you create a Twitter list for all your event participants, then you can then see the Twitter streams of the tweets as they come from all the people in that list.

   This gives you a real time updates on what your group is talking about and what they are interested in discussing online. This is great for customer service so you can address any concerns as they arise and be there for your attendees and all other participants in a timely manner.

You can create different list for different groups of people like a list for attendees, another for speakers, sponsors, exhibitors and panelists, and another one for you staff.

5. Target audience - Do a Twitter search for people using the right and relevant keywords about your event. Follow these people. Learn what they like, what they are talking about, their interests and what they would like to see more of. Go where they are.

6. Welcome attendees by tagging them with @name, their Twitter handles.

7. For your affiliates - Make it easy for them to promote your event by providing them with customized tweets with the event hashtag and your event website link. Give them a variety of differently worded tweets.

8. Make your tweet just under 110 characters, so there's plenty of space for retweeting and tagging or mentioning or giving people credits, if necessary.

9. Promoted tweets - These are paid advertisements.

10. Direct messaging - In February 2015, Twitter unveiled another feature that could be very useful in event marketing. Now you can privately message your event participants.

This is very helpful for last minute event changes or developments that you just want specific people to reach out to.

11. Hashtags

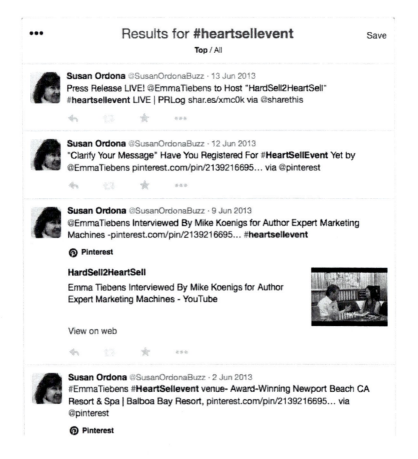

An example of Twitter Event Marketing
(Emma Tiebens' event) with event hashtag

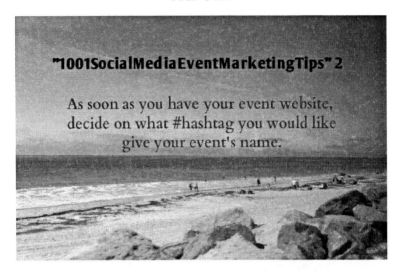

"1001SocialMediaEventMarketingTips" 2

As soon as you have your event website, decide on what #hashtag you would like give your event's name.

According to a survey by Dan Zarella of Hubspot[6], tweets that contain hashtags are 55% more likely to be re-tweeted.

So what is a hashtag? When you see a keyword with a # sign before it, that's a hashtag. It's a very useful search tool. You can search for tweets about your event by searching it with a hashtag. For example, if you want to know all the tweets about a particular event (with their event hashtag), then just type in the hash tag on the search bar. Everyone who is talking about it will show on your Twitter thread.

A typical hashtag should be easy to remember and short, which is great for Twitter since you only have 140 characters total.

There are exceptions to this. When I was researching for the right hashtag for Global Lifestyle Entrepreneur and New

---

[6] "[New Data] Use "Quotes" and #Hashtags to Get More ..." 2013.
<http://danzarrella.com/new-data-use-quotes-and-hashtags-to-get-more-retweets.html>

York Times Best Selling Author Daven Michaels' Beyond Business Live Event, I tried short hashtags that I thought would be relevant to his event. Well, those short ones were already in use and in topics that were nowhere related to Daven's event. To be relevant, we picked #beyondbusinesslive. In this case, it was easy to remember because that's the name of the event and the event website. It became consistent with the hashtags used on Facebook, Instagram, and Google+.

Another example of using a longer hashtag that makes more sense than just a few letters that could easily be pointing to something that is not even related to the keyword, is International Speaker/Author, Internet Marketer Larry Loik's event #dropshiplivepro instead of an acronym.

There's a tool called www.twubs.com where you can search for your hashtag and see if it's available or not. You can register your hashtag, and you will be able to communicate and engage with your network in one hashtag landing page.

A word on Hashtags: I always go easy on hashtags. I don't overuse them. I always have to think about the purpose of having a hashtag by asking myself, is this something that people would be searching for? Then that puts me back to just getting to the basics of relevant keywords to the topic or the event.

Instagram

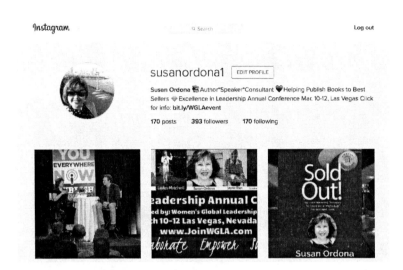

Who isn't on Instagram yet? I first heard of this app at dinner one evening a few years ago. As we chatted with our server, the conversation turned to iPhones, and he told us about this new app called Instagram. I checked it out right away. I loved it then and love it even more now!

With 200 Million monthly active users, 60 million photos posted daily, and an average of 1.6 Billion likes every day, Instagram is one social sharing app that can't be ignored. (Source: Simply Measured).

Instagram is an app that you can download on your iPhone or Android smartphone. It is a fun way to share your photos and up to 15-second videos with family, friends, and your community. You can share images from your camera roll, as well as those you take in real time as they happen.

Tips for Using Instagram to Promote Your Events:

1. On your profile, while you're promoting your event, put your current event website or landing page as your website instead of your main business website, so it goes directly to your event's website. For example, since I'm promoting my book launch, the website is http://SusanOrdonaBook.com

    On the last line of your profile information that describes you, put your Event's name.

An example of an Instagram profile

2. Hashtag - On Instagram, you can put multiple hashtags on your event's post. My recommendation is to create hashtags that are relevant and have the right keywords for your event. My suggestion is not to overdo it. I usually say up to four hashtags on a post is enough. Too many can be so much that it doesn't make sense anymore, meaning the hash-tagged topics are not even ones that someone will be searching for to find you and your event.

3. Tagging- Tag your event's speakers, exhibitors, and other participants.

Time Saving Tip for Instagram

Instagram doesn't have that "square" photo default anymore, so there's more flexibility on the photo sizing now. You can also choose your photo filters to get the impact you want for your photos.

For your event's up to 15-second videos, aside from being able to do the filters, you can also trim and edit your videos.

4. There is a feature, "cover frame," where you can select the thumbnail you want to show on your Instagram feed. Here, choose the thumbnail that shows your event's info to optimize its visibility.

5. Sharing: When you post your Instagram event photo or video, you can post it to your followers or "direct" (direct messaging feature) message to your target audience. This is a big opportunity to reach out, build your list, and increase your subscribers.

6. Sharing avenues: you can share to Facebook, Twitter, Flickr, Email, and Tumblr.

7. You can also copy the link and share.

8. Don't forget your photo map! This points to the location of where the photo or video was taken. This is also great for "during event" posting.

Instagram Shortcuts for Event Marketing:

1. Event website on profile

2. Event's name on profile

3. Event hashtag

4. Tag event's speakers and participants

5. Choose desired filters on your smartphone's camera settings

6. "Cover frame" to select event video's thumbnail

7. Direct messaging for specific event audience

8. Share photos and videos to Facebook

9. Share to Twitter

10. Share to Tumblr

11. Share to Flickr

12. Share to your email list

13. Share the link

14. Activate Photo Map feature to check in on Foursquare

15. Photo map to show your event location

16. Encourage Likes, Comments and Sharing

Pinterest

This platform has 72.5 Million unique visitors in the US alone! 71% are female and 29% are male[7], but don't worry: for you men out there, this gender breakdown will change very soon, as more men are getting into Pinterest.

Pinterest is not only for bridal ideas, recipes, and fashion. It's also great for marketing. There are more and more businesses using Pinterest to showcase their products and services.

I first used Pinterest in the early days to pin visually appealing images of my hobbies and interests. Later on as I was traveling and attending events, I started grouping my pins into boards that are also event-related, like hotels, restaurants, and cities, and it hit me! I can use this to showcase my events and those that I help promote!

So, here are my tips for using Pinterest for event marketing. You can build and implement event boards right away and pin images from your website that are event-related.

---

[7] "The Best Days & Times To Pin On Pinterest | Anna Bennett ..." 2015.
     <https://www.linkedin.com/pulse/best-days-times-pin-pinterest-anna-bennett>

1. On your profile - "About You" is always your prime real estate in social media. In addition to how you help people (that's what you do), you can put your current event's name, date, location, and a brief description along with the title. Make sure not to exceed the 160 characters allowed. You can include the event's website, but it won't be clickable.

An example of a Pinterest profile

2. On your profile, you can put your business website as well. Then when people go to your website, they will see your strategically clickable event's banner or logo, taking them to your event website or landing page.

3. On your settings, under "notifications," you can set your notification settings the way you want. It depends on how much engagement you want to do when you're promoting your event.

   You can be notified in a variety of ways: do you want to get notifications from everyone or only from the people you follow? Do you want to be notified by email, by phone, or both?

On your mobile phone, there are even more ways to interact with people based on how and what you're notified about. We'll discuss more on that later in the mobile marketing section of this book.

4. Add a Pinterest button to both your event website and your main website, so those visitors can connect with you on Pinterest as well.

5. Logging in to Facebook and Twitter from Pinterest. In your account settings, you can set up a connection to Facebook and Twitter. What this does: when you go to your Pinterest profile, you'll see the icons for Facebook and Twitter. When you click the Facebook icon, for example, it will take you to your Facebook account.

6. You can also take advantage of the Rich Pins, which are pins that give you more information about the pin itself. The types of Rich Pins available right now are for movies, products, places, articles, and recipes. The most relevant ones for event marketing are the article and places pins.

The article pin would be good for pinning your event website, while the places pin is great for showing the location of the event, with its map, address, and phone number.

7. Make sure that the first two boards in your Pinterest account are about your event. Not only are they the first ones that appear when someone visits your Pinterest page, but they are also the first two boards that show up on mobile phones.

Some Ideas for Creating Your Event-Related Boards on Pinterest:

- Hotels
- Locations - Cities
- Hotel lobbies
- Hotel Restaurant Culinary treats
- Points of interest nearby

- Attractions
- Hotel amenities
- Speakers
- Books written by the speakers
- Articles/press releases

Sharing Avenues:

- You can copy and paste the link of the whole event board and share.

- You can also copy and paste the link of each individual event pin and share.

- With your event board, you can put your event website on the board description, but it won't be clickable.

- When you create a board and pin from a website, it will have buttons for sharing directly to Twitter and Facebook (you have to activate "post to timeline" for Facebook).

- Pinterest allows you to pin from either a website or from your own images. There are different ways to optimize this. Pin from both your main website (where your event's banner is prominent), and your

SOLD-OUT!

event website. Share images or photos you have that are preferably watermarked with your event website.

Examples of Events on Pinterest

Excellence in Leadership Annual Conference 2016

Women of Wealth and Abundance

YouTube and Video Marketing

With more than 1 billion unique worldwide visitors every month, YouTube remains the biggest and most popular video sharing site. No wonder its role in event marketing is so important—videos can affect us in more engaging ways than just reading a text or looking at a still image. I don't know about you, but when I go to an event website or landing page and there's a short video on their homepage, I am inclined to watch it right away. Videos just capture your attention in a way no other media can.

If you have the budget for professionally-made event marketing videos, by all means, do it. If not, there are less expensive ways to create presentable videos. Nowadays, even your smartphones can produce awesome videos. Sometimes you don't even need a camera crew. You can do a selfie video!

You can create event invitation videos, video interviews of speakers, tips that relate to the topics at the event, a sneak peek at the event venue, or even behind the scenes footage.

What you should include in your short minute videos:

1. Your name and role at the event
2. Name of event
3. Date/dates of event
4. Location
5. Event website
6. Description of the event
7. Why people should attend

How Can I Optimize My Videos On Youtube?

1. Choose your thumbnail or upload your own screenshot of an image that has your event website in it.

2. You can annotate and put text about your event.

3. You can edit your video on Youtube.

4. The Title of Video should have the proper keywords for SEO (search engine optimization) in order to be found easily with a web search.

5. On the first line of the video description, put your event website or landing page (as http://.......), and your main business website (as http://.....).

6. Write a short, keyword-rich, concise description of what your event is all about.

7. Tags - use relevant keywords, such as event name, location-city, hotel, speakers, sponsors, books written by you and the speakers, and your name-- don't forget that!

Where Can I Share My Event Marketing Videos From Youtube For Maximum Exposure?

1. Embed your video in your main website. Write a blog about it, incorporating your video, with the link to your event website.

2. Embed it directly in your event website.

3. Email the link to your family and friends.

4. Include this video in your email newsletter.

5. Share to Facebook.

6. Share to LinkedIn.

7. Share to Twitter.

8. Share to Google +.

9. Pin it to Pinterest.

10. Share to Tumblr, Reddit, and Digg, if applicable.

11. There is another way to share from:

a.	Youtube	e.	Twitter
b.	Your Main website	f.	LinkedIn
c.	Your event website	g.	Google+ 1
d.	Facebook	h.	Pinterest

Tip on Sharing:

When you share a link, be sure to write something that goes with it. It's nice to know what the link is all about. Even if people can see the thumbnail or video on autoplay, provide a short sentence with a description.

Another video sharing site that is worth checking out is Vimeo, which attracts over 100 Million unique visitors per month.

Mobile Marketing

By now, you should have your main business website, event website, and your social media networks already set up and running.

I'm sure you also have your smartphone with you. More than half of all mobile phone users in the world have smartphones. Why? Because we have become a society of "instant" and "now"! We want to consume information right now in real time. We want to know the answers now!

As an event producer, that is what you have to realize that mobile marketing is here! Your attendees have their smartphones with them almost 24/7. AND they want to register at your event now. Are you ready?

What can I do to meet my target audience where they are?

Tips on using mobile marketing for creating the social buzz for your event:

1. Starting with your main website - It should be mobile friendly. People should be able to look at your website in full on their mobile phones.

2. Your event website - Just like your main website, people should be able to see all of your site in full. So make sure that your event website is optimized with all the necessary information about your event. If you meet them where they are, they will click that register button before you know it.

3. Mobile apps - Install the social media apps on the mobile smartphones. They will be handy before, during, and after the event.

Mobile technology makes it so much easier to engage with your attendees on social media on all the social media platforms.

Here are just some of the mobile apps that would be handy for your event marketing:

Facebook	Google+	Flickr
LinkedIn	Google Maps	Scribblelive
Instagram	Foursquare	Eventbrite
Twitter	Tumblr	Evernote
Pinterest	QRreader	AroundMe

How is Pinterest mobile?

On Pinterest, make sure your first two boards are your event boards (and pins). When you create a Pinterest board, usually the newest one goes at the bottom. Drag that to the top left side because on mobile phones the first two boards on your Pinterest account will be the ones you'll see right away.

You'll be notified on your phone of the different ways that people are engaging with you. These notifications are very important as they let you know what's going on that needs your attention. Of course, you chose how engaged you want to be.

You can address all kinds of notifications (for example, about your event) and followers on your account on the go. Do you want to respond when someone repins one of your event pins, follows you or your event boards, mentions you in a comment or in an event pin description, when someone comments on your event pin, when someone (maybe an attendee or potential attendee) sends you a private message, or when a Facebook or Twitter friend (again, an attendee) joins Pinterest, creates a pin or a board? With all notifications like these, being on mobile will allow you to respond to your attendees in a timely manner. You can edit these notifications according to what you think is relevant or not to your event promotion.

Making sure that the first two boards in your Pinterest account are about your event is very important. When someone visits your Pinterest profile on a mobile phone, those two boards are the ones that pop up and are visible right away, so make them all about your event.

QR Codes

Have you noticed those funny-looking, maze-like squares printed in black and white? They are popping up more and more, appearing in places like coupons, advertisements and business cards. The squares are called QR codes, "QR" standing for quick response.

QR codes are marketing tools that make it easier for your businesses to communicate information about anything that you want clients or potential clients to see. Smartphone users scan the codes, which then transports them to the Internet page of your choice. Once generated and set up, QR codes can point to your website, social network profiles such as a Facebook fan page, LinkedIn, Twitter or Pinterest, your YouTube videos, or any other URL you decide.

With the rapid growth of mobile phone users, this scanning technology has profound business potential. Consider this, according to comScore[8], about 20.1 million people scanned QR codes during a three-month average period ending October 2011. QR code scanning is only increasing.

How Do I Get Started Creating the Codes?

Use a QR code generator such as Kaywa (I generate codes using this) and Bitly (when you want to shorten a URL, you can also generate a QR code).

As for QR scanning apps, there are plenty of them out there. Two I recommend are QRReader and Qrafter.

Now that you know where to go to generate a QR code, you need ideas for using them effectively. Here are a few to get your brainstorming started:

- Use a QR code to send out a Tweet.
- Add a QR code to a Wisestamp email signature.
- Place one on name tags given out at live events.
- Use QR codes on social networking sites.
- Put one on your business cards.

---

[8] "20 Million Americans Scanned a QR Code in October ..." 2015. <https://www.comscore.com/Insights/Data-Mine/20-Million-Americans-Scanned-a-QR-Code-in-October>

- Use the codes in magazine, newspaper and other print ads.

- Put a QR code on your luggage tags.

- Display them in store windows.

- Promote an event.

As a final thought, I'll leave you with another idea just to give you a notion of the possibilities that QR codes hold for businesses:

I dined out with my family recently at a local restaurant. We were seated, but it took the server a bit to take our orders, so we were waiting and waiting and, yes, waiting. There were plain paper placemats on the table. You see where I'm going with this? As a marketer, my mind was racing into marketing and information-sharing ideas. QR codes on the placemats would have could have accomplished a lot.

QR Codes Could Have Taken Us To:

- The restaurant's website to get to know more about it

- Their menu so we could have placed our orders

- Photos of their food

- Videos

- Their restaurant's Yelp reviews

- Their Facebook, Twitter, or Pinterest profiles

- A landing page where we could join their mailing list that promotes their restaurant events

Podcasting

What is podcasting? My simple definition of a podcast is one of the digital media in the form of audio (or video) downloaded through iTunes or other internet syndication, that I can listen to whenever I want, wherever I am, and however I want.

It's definitely one on my to-do list.

Podcasting has been around for a while. I first heard the word podcast from Larry Loik, founder of The Real Estate Investor Network (REINCLUB) who was then podcasting about real estate way back in late 2006. With the surfacing of other technologies like the smartphones, I didn't hear much about podcasting until about less than two years ago. Guess what? The podcast audience is growing and growing as more people are jumping into this content distribution channel every day. Podcasting is becoming more and more popular with many well known marketers utilizing this. According to eMarketer, there were 17 million podcast downloads in 2008; it was projected to double in 2013![9]

How Can I Use Podcasting To Get The Word Out About My Events?

If you are also the event host, invite your speakers to be on your show to talk about their topics of expertise. There shouldn't be any mention of the event at this point. They should just be giving pure content. At the end of the podcast

[9] "Podcasting Goes Mainstream - eMarketer." 2013.
<http://www.emarketer.com/Article/Podcasting-Goes-Mainstream/1006937>

episode, you can then talk about their websites or blogs, where they are in social media and any upcoming events where they will speaking at.

Talk about any topic that will be of benefit to your listeners and at the end of the podcast just invite them to go to your event to learn more.

Post your podcast to your website and share it from there. Always link back to your main website where you'll have your event prominently placed.

With a podcast, you're establishing yourself as an authority in whatever niche you are in. People will follow you, subscribe to your podcast, visit your website, connect with you on social networks. If your event is everywhere, people will find themselves attending your events eventually.

Chapter Eight:

Putting It All Together - Your Event Marketing Blueprint

21 Event Marketing Tactics That Will Help You Jumpstart Your Event Marketing:

1. Have clarity as to what you want to accomplish by having an event.

2. Think about whom you want to invite.

3. Get the best deal on your event venue.

4. Go through your email database and identify your target market.

5. Be clear on the topics that you want your audience would be interested in.

6. Think about the demographics of your audience.

7. Take into consideration the time of the year.

8. Start to contact your speaker/speakers.

9. Set price points you want for your event.

10. The layout of the event website has to be brainstormed by now.

11. Look at the colors, fonts and the design of your event website.

12. Make sure of your event location, for example the city where you want it held.

13. Set up Facebook Personal Profile.

14. Set Up Facebook Fan Page.

15. Set up a Facebook Event Page.

16. Create a Twitter account.

17. Create a hashtag for your event.

18. If the event is big enough, set up its own Twitter account with its own Twitter handle.

19. Set up a LinkedIn profile.

20. Create a LinkedIn company page.

21. Take a deep breath and start your Event Mindmap strategy.

There are still many things we can do for our events. So many tools and strategies - the most important is to apply those that are relevant to what your event is all about.

Engagement, Engagement, Engagement— Before, During, and After the Event

When I was growing up in the Philippines, I often heard the word "Smorgasbord", a Scandinavian term for buffet as we know it here in the US. Don't ask me how that word became popular with Filipinos, but somehow that's what we called buffets back then.

Anyway, as we're talking here about marketing tools, platforms, channels, tips and strategies, I liken them to a "Smorgasbord", where you can pick and choose what you want to apply to your event. In event marketing, there's no "one size fits all" since every event is different.

Timelines for event marketing also change with different events. Usually 3-6 months would be ideal as planning ahead of time and early on is better than trying to fit everything in 30 days or less.

Social media is based on engagement and relationships, which take a lot of time to develop for people to like, trust, and do business with you or attend your events. It's like dating someone. Relationships usually don't happen overnight. Of course, there are rare exceptions.

It's a different story if you already have long term relationships with your target audience, your event marketing timeline maybe shorter as you already have an audience waiting for you. They already know you, like you, and trust you. If you have a small intimate group of people, that timeline may even be shorter.

You want to play safe and set the timeline for 2-6 months to give you plenty of time to do the whole event marketing process.

Tip: Encourage your attendees and all event participants to go mobile, by installing all the social media apps (Facebook, LinkedIn, Twitter, Pinterest, Instagram, Youtube, Google+, Hootsuite, etc.) that they are going to use during your event process.

Before Event - Create The Buzz

1. Email marketing system in place and utilizing:

   - Email Newsletter with WiseStamp Email Signature

   - WiseStamp Event Promoter tool

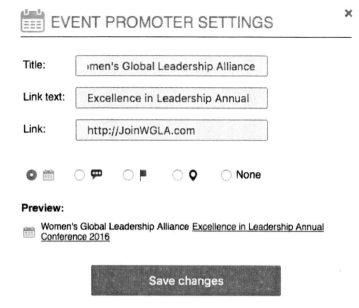

2. Main website in place

3. Social media accounts set up or refreshed and optimized

- Facebook
- Twitter
- Instagram -mobile
- Pinterest
- Youtube
- Vimeo - if desired
- LinkedIn - if desired
- Google + - if desired
- Flickr - if desired

4. Send Save The Date announcements

5. Event Hashtag

6. Assemble Event Team

   - Social Media Manager - social media planning and implementation
   - Photographer
   - Videographer
   - Graphic designer
   - Web developer

7. Start Working on Event website/landing page/Online Event Registration sites (Eventbrite or EventSpot)

8. Contact speakers, sponsors, exhibitors, panelists, and circle of influence

9. Contact family and friends by word of mouth

10. Email database

11. Content - current ones and from past events. Repurpose your content!

    - photos/images
    - videos/ YouTube
    - articles/blogs
    - social media swipes
    - audio

12. Tools to create images:

   - www.Canva.com

   - www.shareasimage.com

   - www.picmonkey.com

   - www.Wordswag.co

13. Facebook Event Page/Facebook Groups/Facebook Ads

14. LinkedIn groups (relevant to your event topics)/Linked Ads

15. Twitter /Twitter List/ Promoted Tweets

16. Instagram/Pinterest/Vine

17. Press release - 1 week before the event

18. Google+ Event Page - 1200 x 300 pixel

   Utilize Google hangouts on air to do a pre-event conversation with your attendees and other event participants.

19. Start your "Content Dripping" to different social media sites like Facebook, Twitter, LinkedIn, Instagram, Pinterest, Google+, Youtube.

20. Set up Hootsuite as a social media management tool as well as scheduling your posts or updates.

21. Promote your speakers: Give your attendees reasons why they should attend because of what the speaker is going to

share with them. Highlight your speakers. Share their success stories as well as their challenges and how they overcame those hurdles.

Weeks before the event from the time that everything is in place, all of these processes should be going on too: Continue "Content Dripping": Continue engaging with your social media networks.

This is an example of an event campaign that Life and Image Reinvention Authority, Motivational EDUtainer, TV Host, Author & Speaker and Event Organizer did for her own event, Ferlie Almonte (www.UnleashyourBling.com).

Some of the event marketing strategies "Unleash Your B.L.I.N.G." event:

1. Hired a web developer - who wrote a sales page with a video, which attracted 50% of her attendees. A mobile app enhanced the effectiveness of the sales page.

2. Social media channel - mainly Facebook

3. Reached out to people she already knew - local friends, community leaders- by personal phone calls and private messages.

Always Promote Your Speakers!

Your speakers are a mountain of information, especially with their expertise in the topics that they will talk about at your event. With that alone, you'll have plenty of content to share in your social media networks.

This is an interview I did with one of my clients and also my coach/mentor, Larry Loik, an international speaker, author and internet marketer as we were preparing for his VIP Speaker Bootcamp.

These Are His Best "Speaking Business" Tips:

Tip #1 – Have a solid contract to protect you. If you're flying from out of town and the promoter promises you 300 people and there's only 30 people, put it in your clause that if there's just a certain amount of people, at least your travel expenses are covered, you get an upfront fee, or you get a higher percentage split on the back end...make sure that you're covered on that as well.

If it's possible, request to process the credit cards of your sales yourself rather than the promoter. If you trust the promoter a lot, that's great, but put it in the clause as well that you get paid within 30 days with a maximum 45 days.

Tip #2 – Is it better to have a physical product or a digital product? Larry's answer is: Both! People like to have something tangible in their hands like a CD or DVD in a nice case. Something easy to carry or transport if they're traveling. The rest can be downloaded digitally via drip campaign or all at once. The trend is digital, but at least give your clients something they can walk away with.

Tip #3 – When you think about speaking, it's not just speaking from the stage, but also a 1 on 1 speaking with people. It's also about negotiation, techniques, strategies, closing, mindset, topics, how to get yourself on stages, what to do at an event, how to follow up after an event, how to deal with promoters, how to choose an event, what cities to speak at, structuring your offer and your presentation.

Tip #4 – Should you speak at a free event or paid event? YES to both. Craft your offer to match with your audience. If you are in a multi-speaker event, look at the price points of the other speakers as well so your offers are not overpriced or underpriced.

Tip #5 – Closing Technique: When you get off stage, walk straight to the sales table. Tell the people who are asking you questions to follow you to the back table so you can answer questions for everybody. Go behind the sales table to draw people there. Tell the promoter to keep your mic on so you'll be answering questions that are also in the minds of other people.

The Importance of Speakers at Events: How To Introduce and Welcome a Speaker

You know that Event Speakers are big attractions at your event, so you should promote them really well.

Here are some insights on how introduce and welcome speakers the right way so that they will come back to speak and draw the crowd for you:

1. Energy is very important! Build that energy before hand, so when it's time for the introducer to introduce the speaker, there's already that momentum going.

2. Get everybody in the room before the introducer and the speaker get on stage.

3. Choice of music at an event plays an important role in keeping that energy up before the introducer and the speaker go up the stage. Choose event appropriate music.

4. Close the doors to filter outside noise.

5. For the speakers, there should be a prepared written introduction. If there's anyone who knows you well, it's you.

6. Speakers shouldn't assume that the introducer has all the necessary information about you from your website or any other sources. Make it easier for the introducer to do the job and also to avoid misrepresentation of you because of inaccurate information about you.

7. Some speakers have a carefully scripted and prepared video introduction of themselves that showcases them and their beginnings, credentials and accomplishments with a compelling musical background that builds up the excitement, especially towards the end of the video. These intro videos take the place of an introducer in many cases.

8. If there is a need for someone to introduce the speaker, here are some pointers for introducers. The introducer has to already have a relationship with the speaker ahead of time so that there's a personal connection present right in that moment. Whether it's a phone call, meeting and knowing the speaker before the event, or spending a few minutes with the speaker before stage time, getting that personal connection is important.

9. Do a research of the speaker. Get a hold of the bio, go to the website, do a Google search. By doing so, you'll get a feel of the whole picture.

10. Ask the speaker about his/her topic and if there's anything that is relevant that he/she wants to be included in the introduction.

11. The introducer has to practice the introduction ahead of time, whether it's a written one or an ad-libbed intro. Reading an introduction is alright and so is glancing at your notes, but it is even better if you can connect and look at your audience.

12. Make the introduction brief and concise. One to three minutes is enough so you don't take up too much of the speaker's stage time.

13. As you are the link from the audience to the speaker, an introducer's job is very important. So dress and act the part, you are a speaker yourself!

During Event - Showtime More Buzz

It's show time! It's also the height of the excitement in the event process! This is when we, as event organizers and marketers, are engaging with our attendees, speakers, panelists, sponsors, exhibitors, and event staff in real time and in a real atmosphere. We are interacting directly, sharing all our messages to different channels!

To share the event experience with people who couldn't attend, encourage attendees to tweet during the event, along with sharing messages on social media about the event (with the event hashtag).

1. Make sure there's a wireless connection (enough Wi-Fi bandwidth) for everyone at the event so they can easily share the event experience via social media. Today, that is a necessity. There were a few times that I couldn't do the social media sharing at an event I was covering because of the lack of Wi-Fi bandwidth.

2. Event Hashtag – it should visible everywhere for all event participants. It should be on the big screen.

3. Social media correspondent - if applicable. Candid interviews with attendees, speakers, sponsors, exhibitors. I personally love to interview people on the spot just like a "red carpet" candid spontaneous short video interview with selfie video interviewing style.

    Take the opportunity to interview the speakers or the key players at events. You can do this! Just be friendly, quick and approach them with a big smile and thank them for what they share at the events.

4. Social media manager - live tweeting, live Facebook posting and sharing of photos and videos, monitor event hashtag, groups.

5. Take photos - lots of them! Candid photos (not unflattering) are best. Use judgment when sharing photos and videos.

6. Audience on their smartphones? Take that moment to tweet something they just learned from the event. Of course, include the event hashtag and tag the speakers and their friends.

7. Selfie time! Take selfie photos and videos. I do a lot of selfie shots and videos because it is faster for me to do my job. I don't have to wait for someone to take my photos and I know exactly how I would look like in the photos, eliminating additional shots.

8. How about putting the event's Instagram photos or Twitter stream on the big screen on break times? People always get excited when they see their photos and their tweets on the big screen. Encourage the event team to participate whenever they can to social media postings.

9. Take videos - take videos at live events during breaks and networking parties. Interview event participants. Post on YouTube and other social networking sites.

10. Livestream - those are short live videos streamlined on real time. For people not at the event, this creates excitement and make them want to be at the event or at the next one. It makes them say, "I better not miss their next event".

11. Live tweeting - Tweeting right there from the event! Don't forget your event Hashtag. Tag(if it's ok) relevant people in your tweets. As you're monitoring your Twitter feed, retweet someone's tweet that you want to share to your followers. Reply to comments or questions.

12. Live blogging - Scribblelive is a live blogging platform. Writing a blog even if it's a short article takes time. If you're going to use this, it's better to have one designated person do this.

13. Live Facebook - yes, live Facebook posts. Remember your hashtags and tagging.

14. Live Instagram - yes, Instagram posts as well, with hashtag and tagging. Don't forget your 15-sec. videos!

15. Vine videos - these are 6-sec. videos that are constantly looping. What's great about this is that your Vine video link can be seen on Twitter now on your profile.

16. Red Carpet photo opportunity Red Carpet experience with Speaker, Author, and Magnetic Marketing Expert, Emma Tiebens and Nellie Reyes Schwab, an Innovative Consultant at Lanelle Synergy Business Solutions.

17. Get the audience involved - attendees nowadays want to get involved, whether it's dancing on stage, taking pictures, taking videos, they want to be in your show! Get them excited. They are your celebrities!

18. Speakers, sponsors, exhibitors, panelists, entertainers: act like celebrities because you ARE! Stick around, network, have photos or videos taken with the attendees. You want exposure and publicity? This is it! Do you know where those photos are going to be shared, with you tagged and hash-tagged? Social media as a whole is your publicist!

My Personal "During Event" Social Media Tips:

I want to share with you a little bit about multitasking while at events. Here are some of my strategies:

1. Have a mobile device – I know it's basic and overlooked a lot, but it helps.

2. Before the live event, make sure you have created profiles on the social media networks that you like.

3. Be sure to install the social network applications on your mobile device that you would like to use to share your posts. It could be Twitter, Facebook, Pinterest, LinkedIn, etc. or a social media management tool like Hootsuite. (Be sure to upload your photo on these social media network profiles).

4. See to it that you have a fully charged mobile device or keep charging it so you don't run out of battery and thus miss a photo opportunity.

5. Before you start taking photos and posting your updates, you should know the live event's hashtag, and the organizers' names, get to know the speakers, sponsors,

exhibitors, panelists, attendees and their Twitter handles so you can tag them.

6. You can also quote inspiring, informational or motivational phrases and sentences from the speakers and attendees.

7. You can post these one by one to the social networks you like or you can just go to Hootsuite, upload and share your updates or postings with Twitter, Facebook, Facebook Fan Pages, Google +, LinkedIn and check-in at Foursquare with just one click.

Now you're ready to post and share with your social media network friends.

What Do I Post?

I am really into visual content, so I take candid or posed photos and videos first and then include short little captions of what or who to describe your images and videos.

Take those photos, shoot those very short videos (like the 6 sec. videos using Vine), and share! (By the way, it won't hurt to bring extra cameras and batteries)

Most important is to have fun sharing and socializing with your friends at the event!

After Event - Still The Buzz

Your event is over, or is it? Of course not.

Have you ever been to a live event where you wrote so many notes, but couldn't seem to organize them? You probably won't remember much of your scribblings.

For you, as the event organizer, think about connecting more with your attendees. Help them remember your event. The engagement continues!

1. Always remember the event hashtag! Include it in all your social media sharing about your event.

2. Tag, tag, tag your event participants relevant to all your photos, articles/ blogs, posts and videos.

3. Give your attendees the highlights of your event.

4. Share with your attendees a list of resource tools mentioned at the event.

5. Write blog posts/articles to summarize the event.

6. Give your attendees your event's key takeaways in form of videos and blogs.

7. Upload videos to Youtube and Vimeo and share them with your attendees and participants, via social media sites and don't forget to tag them.

8. Upload photos to Flickr. Photos can be shared all at once as an album or "content-dripped" by sharing one by one from the album.

9. Upload photos in album on Facebook. They can be shared as an album or one by one.

10. Send a feedback request to all the attendees.

11. Don't forget to thank your attendees, speakers, sponsors, exhibitors, panelists, and everyone involved with the event.

- Send thank you notes with your letterhead with your information(website, telephone,etc.) and ways to connect with you on Social Media

- Thank them on Social Media where they are - their friends will see your Thank You! They will be curious!

- Write a blog post to thank everyone! Social sharing to the social networks where your attendees are.

- Send Thank You emails to your attendees. Utilize Wisestamp (http://Wisestamp.com) in your email signature so your attendees have another ways to connect more with you.

Doing these things will not only create "buzz" for your event, but they will greatly increase the engagement of the attendees. Remember that the people attending events are so caught up in the event that they forget to capture the moment, and you get the fun and rewarding job of creating a feeling of specialness about your event.

Conclusion

After you have completed your big event, what's next?

Engagement is the key! Whether you have an event or not at the moment, you have to continue engaging with your attendees, customers, and peers. Provide content of value to support them. Relationships with your attendees do not stop just because your event ended. Continue the conversations.

Leverage technology to do that!

If you have high expectations of your own event, know that the audience's expectations of live events are even higher, so be prepared to meet them.

Keep yourself updated with social media, new trends, what network doesn't work anymore, news of the industry and what's coming!

Think as an attendee!

As one who had been involved and had helped in event planning, events set up, event promotions and marketing, managing social media during events, and engaging with attendees after events and ending up developing friendships and long term relationships and social currency, there is so much that goes behind the scenes to put up a memorable live event. It is a big undertaking.

From all the sleepless nights, stressful days, long hours of preparation, the rewards are when you see happy, excited, and "couldn't wait" attendees waiting for the door to open to get the best seats at your event!

They are there because of all those channels of communication - the powerful social media buzz you created that attracted them to fill the seats at your "Sold Out" event!

Acknowledgements

What would I be without YOU?

Yes, without you, there would be no book.

To my husband Roger who has been a pillar of strength for me, my anchor, my unconditional love, my cheerleader, my home, my safe haven, my inspiration...my everything in whatever I do....thank you for being there for me unconditionally.

To my son Andrew, thank you for inspiring me to believe that anything is possible when we want it bad enough. Dare to dream, follow your passion, work hard to get there, and never give up. We (your Dad and I) are here to support you every step of the way! If your 60 year old Mom with no background in book writing can be a #1 Best Selling Author, imagine the possibilities! The world is your oyster, my dearest Andrew!

To my Mom Josefa (Jep), I've always loved you unconditionally. You inspired me with the power of never giving up on giving unconditional love.

To my Papa Eddie, you treated me like your own daughter. Thank you for my formal education; I wouldn't be where I am if not for you and Mom.

To my second Mom, Mama Nating, who raised me and instilled life values that I still look up to, the greatest one being forgiveness...how to forgive someone even when it's very difficult to do so. Thank you for being overprotective of me as if I was the most precious princess in the world.

To my Dad, Lee, thank you for always loving me and my own family all this time despite the distance and time between us. You, Mom Norma, and the whole family are part of my life.

To my parents-in-law, Mom Segunda and Dad Jesus, who were always there for me. I wish you were still here to see me reaching those dreams and putting my passions into realities.

To the Ordona families; my siblings from Mom's side: ChrisAnn, Charles, and George and families; my siblings from Dad's side: Joel, Grace, Ronnie, Lee, Jason, Natly, Sherrie and Dennis and families...you all complete my family circle. Thank you for calling me Ate (older sister). You are part of who I am.

To my extended families, the Almendras, the Katindoys, the Nocetes, the Mandias, the Robins, the Ritagas - thank you for being in the "The Village Who Raised Me" (the families that embraced me and made an impact in my life).

To my dear friend and coach/mentor, Larry Loik, for always believing in me, even when I didn't. Thank you for never giving up on me even when there were many "almost" moments and for pushing me to do something to share my gifts to the world.

To my dear Miss "Clarity Coach" Emma Tiebens, for being there for me as a friend and as a coach, holding my hand up to the fruition of this book, and never letting me fall off the tracks. You just know how to get those ideas out of my head by asking the right questions. No wonder you are my Miss Clarity Coach, because you are! I can't thank you enough.

To my dear friends (I wish I could name all of you) that keep cheering me on and encouraging me while providing the "shoulders to cry on" when I need it. Thank you from my heart.

Thank you to ALL of the speakers, coaches, mentors, teachers, trainers, and event organizers I have been blessed to know! Many of you have now become my dear friends. I thank you for all the great messages that you continue to share, impacting people's lives all over the world. You are the reason why I chose this book topic. The collective knowledge, ideas, and experiences need to be seen, heard, and experienced in all corners of the globe!

To ALL of you, who inspired me and who in one way or another have contributed to the making and success of this book, I am forever grateful!

To those who have ever dreamed of doing something different, those who ever thought of re-discovering your unique gifts, re-visiting your passions, and re-inventing your life, and are bouncing back...you can do it! Just believe in yourself and your uniqueness.

Remember, you are somebody!

And to YOU, the reader of my book! I'm very grateful and humbled by your support in making my book an Amazon #1 Best Seller! You inspire me to continue my journey. Thank you.

Susan

About The Author

Susan is a Speaker, a two time #1 Amazon Best Selling Author, and Book Publishing Consultant. She has mentored and helped clients to self-publish books, which became #1 Best Sellers, using a proven step-by-step system that enables her to help more authors launch their books to  become Best Sellers so they can make more sales, grow their businesses, and be recognized authorities.

In her first Best Seller, *Sold Out: Top Event Marketing Strategies To Create Social Media Buzz For Your Next Event*, she shares her expertise in Event Marketing. Her passion for live event coverage as a Social Media Correspondent and Social Media Event Marketing Strategist to some of the world's high profile Speakers, Experts, Authors, Consultants, and Event Producers makes her the definitive logical choice and expert in creating the Social Media Buzz for many of the industry's top live and virtual events.

Susan's second Best Seller is *Social Buzz For Book: 101 Marketing Strategies To Launch Your Book To A Best Seller So You Can Make More Sales, Grow Your Business, and Become THE Go-to Authority.* In it, she writes about ways and tips that help authors launch their books to become Best Sellers.

Trained as a Clinical Laboratory Scientist with over thirty years of experience in the clinical pathology laboratory setting, Susan Ordona has emerged and reinvented herself following her passion in business and entrepreneurship.

Susan is originally from the Philippines. Before moving to the USA, she was working in a German hospital after graduation from college. It was in Germany where she met and married a young US Army Lieutenant. Since then, the beautiful USA has been her home with her husband, her son, and their little dog, Mia.

Visit www.SusanOrdona.com

www.Facebook.com/SusanOrdona.SocialBuzzForBiz

www.Facebook.com/SusanOrdona

www.Linkedin.com/in/SusanOrdona

www.Twitter.com/SusanOrdonaBuzz

www.instagram.com/susanordona1

www.Pinterest.com/SusanOrdona

www.plus.Google.com/+SusanOrdona

www.YouTube.com/SusanOrdona